AF338128

WAVE HI AND GOODBYE TO ENERGY!

AN INTRODUCTION TO WAVES

PHYSICS LESSONS FOR KIDS
CHILDREN'S PHYSICS BOOKS

What is the first thing you think of when you hear the word "wave"? More than likely the it's either moving your hand in a motion to say hello or the motion of the water moving in the ocean and landing on the beach. However, in this book, you will be learning the meaning of wave as it has to do with physics.

WHAT IS A WAVE?

In physics, a wave is a disturbance traveling through matter and space that transfers energy from one location to another. As you are learning about waves, you must remember that it is a transfer of energy, not of matter.

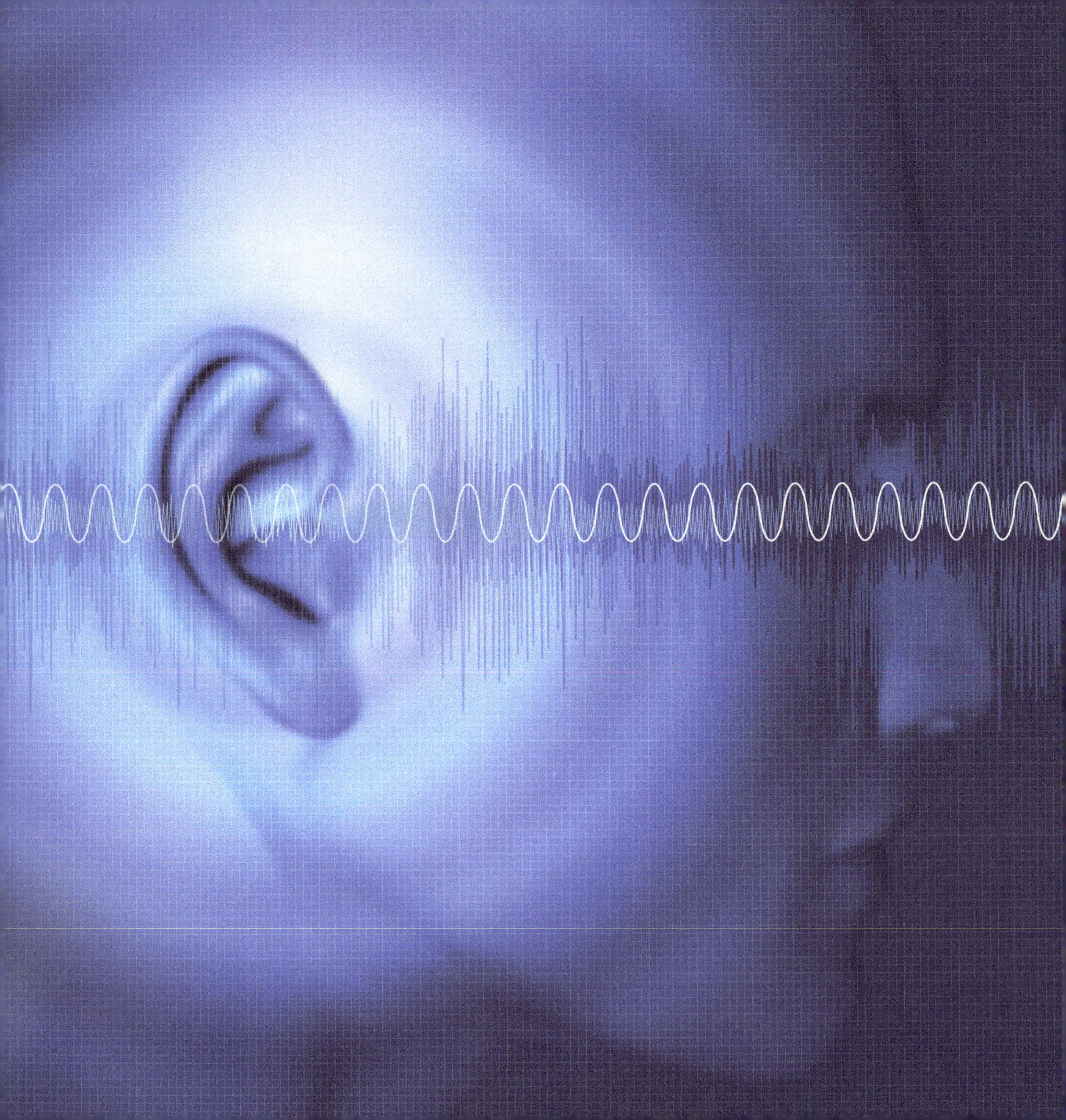

Waves as Seen In Everyday Life

Waves surround us every day. A form of wave that is able to move through matter resulting in a vibration of our eardrums so that we can hear is known as a sound wave.

A light wave is a special type that consists of photons.

If you drop something into a lake you will see waves created in the water. Waves are also used to cook our food fast (microwaves).

TYPES OF WAVES

There are several categories of wave that are dependent upon its characteristics. Read further to learn about terms scientists use in describing waves.

MECHANICAL AND ELECTROMAGNETIC WAVES

Waves are all categorized as being either electromagnetic or mechanical.

Mechanical waves need a medium. They need some type of matter (medium) for traveling. They travel as molecules collide in a medium, and pass the energy. Sound is a perfect illustration of a mechanical wave. It travels through water, air, or solids; however, it cannot travel through a vacuum. It must have a medium to travel. Some other examples are seismic waves, water waves, and waves moving in a spring.

WHAT IS AN ELECTROMAGNETIC WAVE?

Waves that are able to travel through an empty space (vacuum) are known as electromagnetic waves. They move through magnetic and electrical fields generated by charged particles. Some examples of electromagnetic waves are X-rays, radio waves, microwaves and light.

Electromagnetic waves are categorized in accordance to their frequency. Different types have different functions and uses in everyday lives. The most significant of these uses is visible light, which provides us with light so that we can see.

A radio wave has the longest wavelength of all of the waves that are electromagnetic. They range from about a foot long up to many miles long. They are used often for transmitting data and are used for several types of applications that include computer networks, radar, satellites, and radio.

WHAT IS A MICROWAVE?

A microwave is shorter than a radio wave and are measured using centimeters. We use them for transmitting information, cooking food, and with radar helping weather prediction. They are also helpful with communication since they are able to penetrate smoke, clouds and light rain.

SATELLITE DISH TRANSFER DATA

BIG BANG

Our universe contains cosmic background radiation and scientists believe that this may provide clues to the origin of our universe, which they refer to as the Big Bang.

WHAT IS AN INFRARED WAVE?

Infrared waves are between microwaves and visible light waves. They are often classified as "far" infrared and "near" infrared.

BAR CODE SCANNER

Near infrared waves are the ones closer to visible light in wavelength. These are used to change channels with your TV remote control.

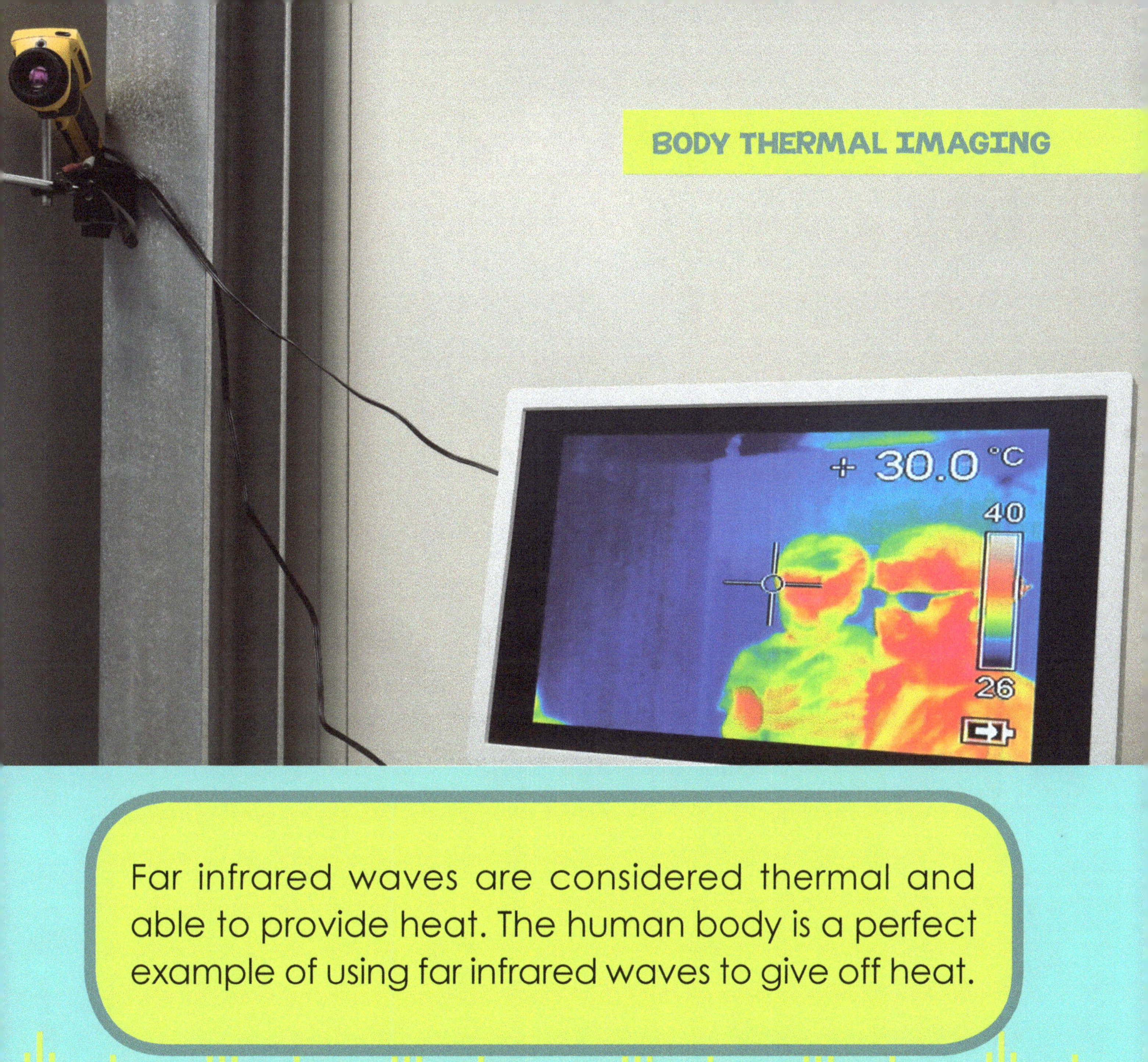

Far infrared waves are considered thermal and able to provide heat. The human body is a perfect example of using far infrared waves to give off heat.

WHAT IS THE VISIBLE LIGHT SPECTRUM?

The visible light spectrum covers wavelengths that are able to be seen by our eyes. The range of this wavelength is from 390 to 700 nm corresponding to frequencies of 430-790 THz.

VISIBLE AND INVISIBLE LIGHT

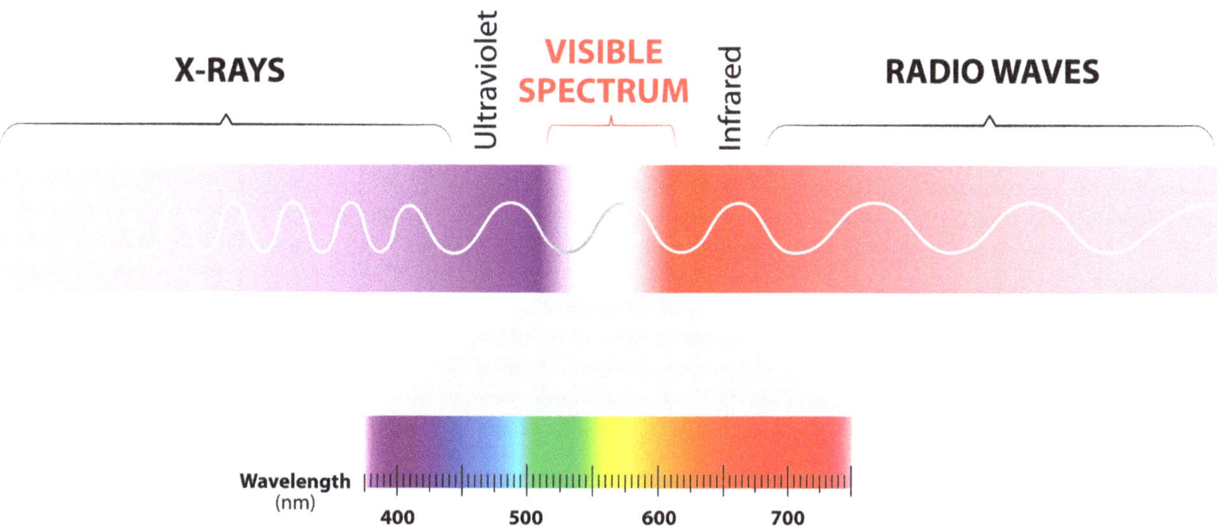

WHAT IS AN ULTRAVIOLET WAVE?

Ultraviolet waves consist of the shortest wavelength following the visible live wave. Sunburns are the result of ultraviolet rays from the sun. The ozone layer protects us from these rays.

Bumblebees are one of a few insects that have the ability to see ultraviolet light. It is also used by powerful telescopes such as the Hubble Space Telescope to see stars that are far way in space.

WILHELM ROENTGEN

X-rays contain shorter wavelengths than ultraviolet rays do. Scientists start to think of these as particles more than waves. They were discovered by Wilhelm Roentgen, a German scientist.

They are able to penetrate soft tissue like muscle and skin and are useful for taking X-ray pictures of bones for medical use.

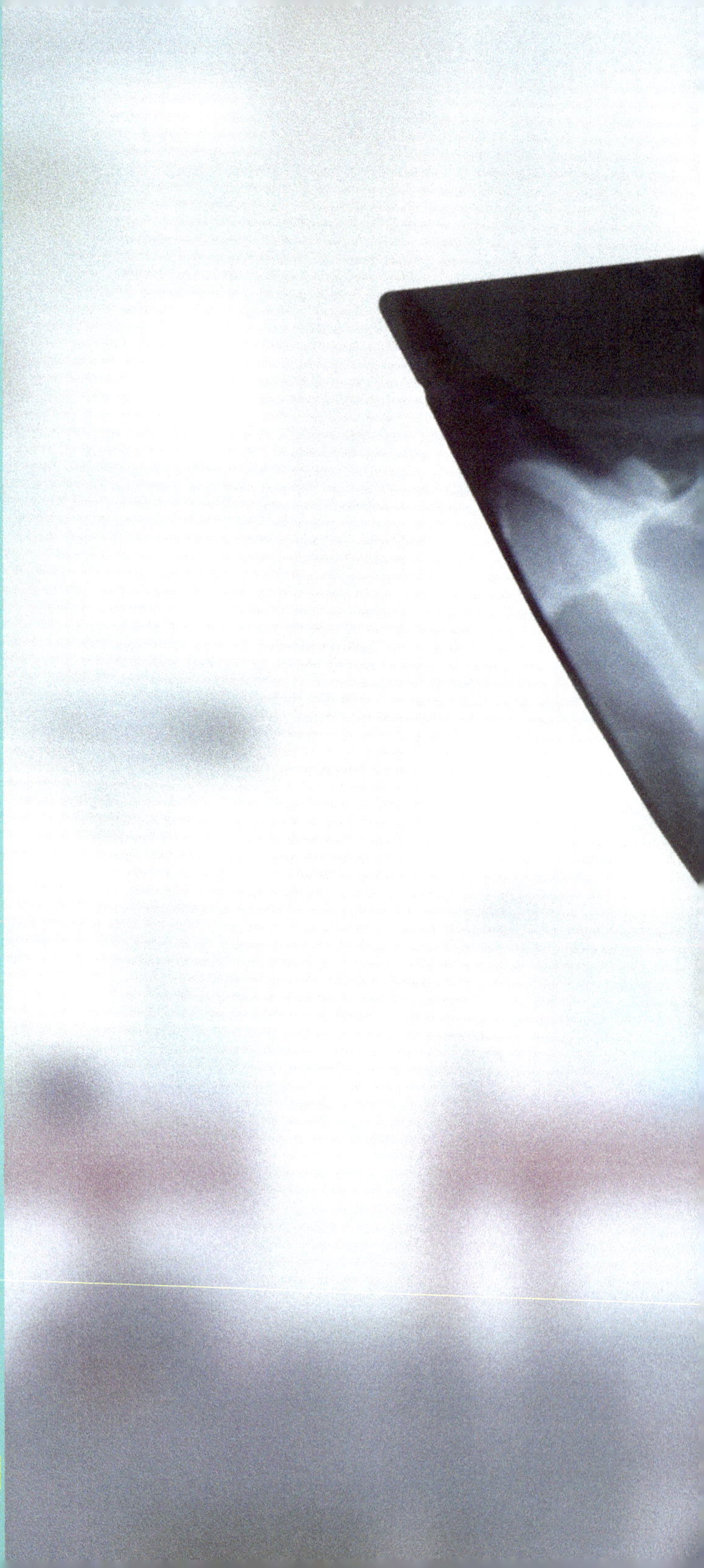

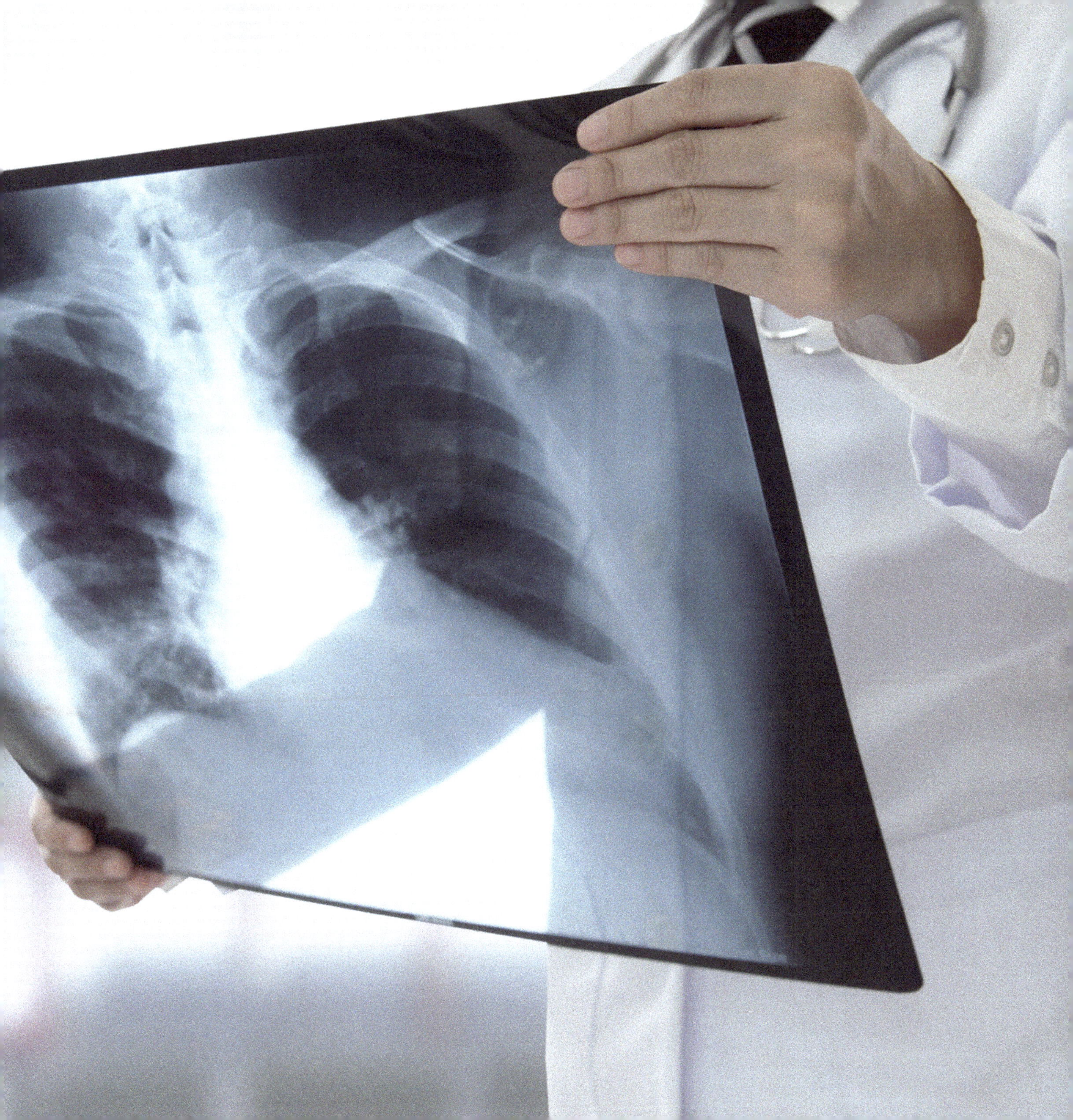

COLLIMATOR RTN
COLL Y1   FIELD Y   COLL Y2
COLL X1   FIELD X   COLL X2
GANTRY RTN
RADIOTHERAPY ACCELERATOR
RADIOTHERAPY SIMULATOR

WHAT IS A GAMMA RAY?

As the wavelengths get shorter, the energy of the electromagnetic waves increases. Gamma rays are the shortest waves and have the most energy. They are sometimes used to treat cancer as well as to take images for diagnostic medicine. They are produced in supernovas and high energy nuclear explosions.

WHAT IS A SUPERNOVA?

A star that explodes is referred to as a supernova and is the biggest explosion that occurs in space. This occurs when there is a change in the center (core) of a star. This change is able to occur in a couple of different ways, and both result in the supernova.

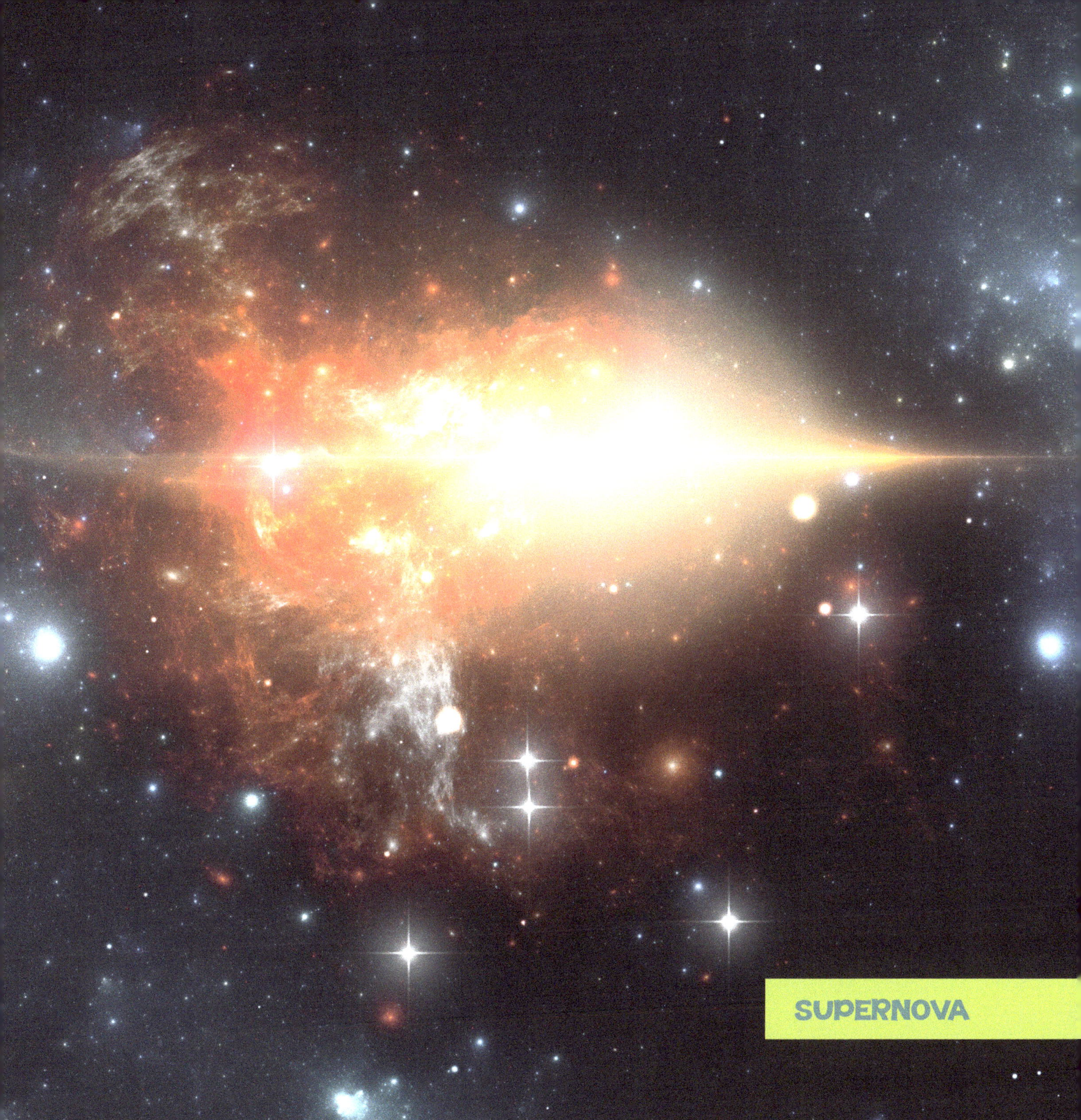
SUPERNOVA

OZONE LAYER

WHAT IS THE OZONE LAYER?

The stratosphere, which is located way up in the Earth's atmosphere, contains a high concentration consisting of ozone molecules formed as the sun hits the oxygen molecules. This is known as the ozone layer.

The direction that the disturbance is traveling is another way to define a wave.

Transverse waves occur when the disturbance moves in a perpendicular direction to the wave. Think of a wave moving from left to right, and the disturbance is moving up and down.

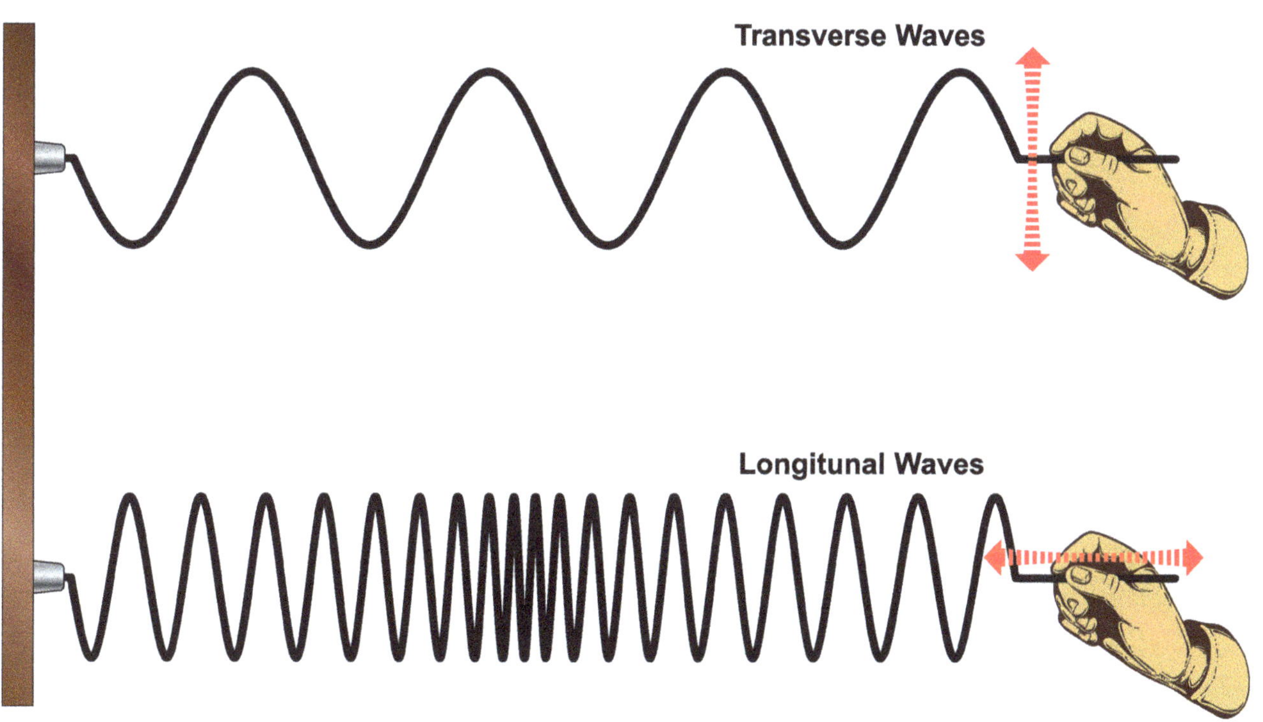

Transverse Waves
Longitunal Waves

An example of a wave that is transvers would be a water wave when the water is moving up and down as the wave is passing through the ocean. Another example would be a wave of fans at a stadium cheering their team (they are moving up and down as the waves travels around the stadium).

Longitudinal waves occur when the disturbance is moving in the same direction as the wave is. An example would be a wave as it moves through a slinky or spring that is stretched out. If a portion of the slinky is compressed, then let go, the wave moves from left to right. The disturbance (the coils of the springs as they move), at the same time, also moves from left to right.

KID PLAYING SLINKY

Sound is another example of a longitudinal wave. When sound waves are broadcast through the medium, molecules collide in the same direction as the sound moves. Sometimes, the molecules get bunched together and this is known as compression, whereas a refraction occurs when the molecules are spread out.

WHAT ARE SOUND WAVES?

A certain type of wave that can be detected by a human ear is a sound wave. They consist of certain characteristics making them unique.

WHAT ARE MECHANICAL WAVES?

An important characteristic of a sound wave is that they are considered to be mechanical waves, meaning that they move through a medium. A sound wave is able to travel through all types of mediums. Typically, we are able to hear sound waves traveling through air, but sound is also able to move through wood, water, the Earth, and several other substances. However, sound is not able to travel through outer space, which is a vacuum. Something that vibrates creates the source for a sound wave. The vibration creates disturbances in the molecules surrounding the source. The wave's energy transfers from one molecule to another in its medium.

FREQUENCY AND PERIOD

A wave's frequency is the number of times that a wave cycles per second. It is measuring using Hertz or cycles per second and is often known by the lower case "f".

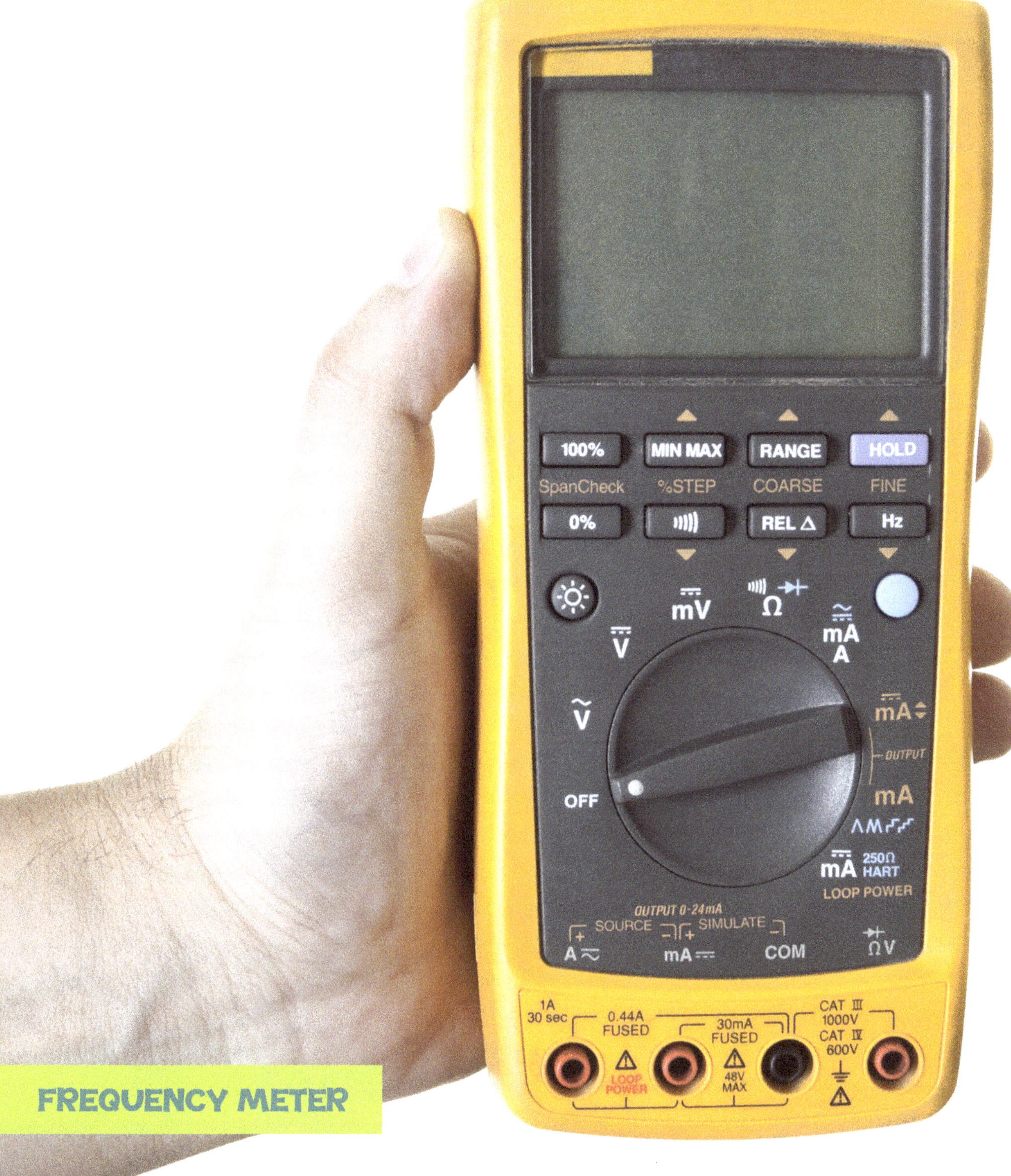

FREQUENCY METER

PENDULUM

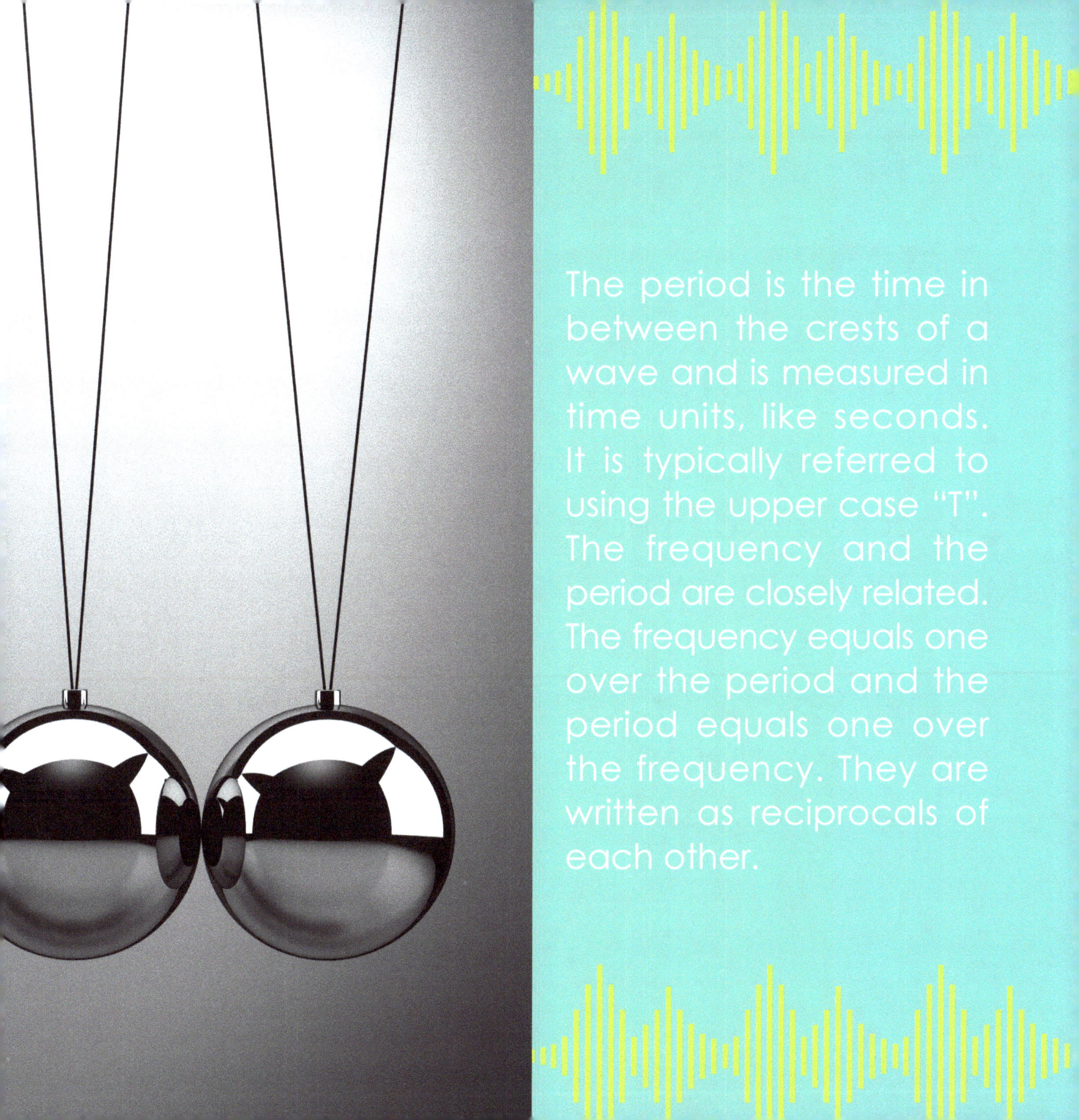

The period is the time in between the crests of a wave and is measured in time units, like seconds. It is typically referred to using the upper case "T". The frequency and the period are closely related. The frequency equals one over the period and the period equals one over the frequency. They are written as reciprocals of each other.

WAVELENGTH

This is the distance between two points that correspond to each other on back-to-back cycles of the wave. It is measured between the two crests or troughs of the wave. It is typically represented by the Greek Letter lambda (λ) in the world of physics.

Did you know there were so many types of waves? Think about all the ways that you can notice these waves in everyday life. Check out the microwave the next time you use it to heat something. Think about it the next time you have to have an X-ray. Think about it when you hear or see something. And, if you are near a beach, check out the waves of the ocean. Think about what is actually happening.

You can learn more about waves as they are used in physics by reading up on them at your local library, researching the internet, and asking questions in your science class!

Visit
BABY PROFESSOR
EDUCATION KIDS
www.BabyProfessorBooks.com
to download Free Baby Professor eBooks and view
our catalog of new and exciting Children's Books